KRYPTO

The SUPERDOG

SUPERMAN CREATED BY
JERRY SIEGEL AND JOE SHUSTER
BY SPECIAL ARRANGEMENT WITH
THE JERRY SIEGEL FAMILY

Raintree is an imprint of Capstone Global
Library Limited, a company incorporated
in England and Wales having its registered
office at 7 Pilgrim Street, London, EC4V
6LB – Registered company number: 6695582

First published by Raintree in 2014
The moral rights of the proprietor have
been asserted.

Originally published by DC Comics in the
US in single magazine form as Krypto The
Superdog #6.

Ashley C. Andersen Zantop Publisher
Michael Dahl Editorial Director
Donald Lemke & Sean Tulien Editors
Bob Lentz Art Director
Hilary Wacholz Designer

DC COMICS
Kristy Quinn Original US Editor

ISBN 978 1 406 27955 9
Printed in China by Nordica.
1013/CA21301918
17 16 15 14 13
10 9 8 7 6 5 4 3 2 1

British Library Cataloguing in Publication
Data
A full catalogue record for this book is
available from the British Library.

KRYPTO

THE SUPERDOG™

Houndin' the Mail Carrier!

JESSE LEON MCCANN....................................WRITER
MIN S. KU ....PENCILLER
JEFF ALBRECHT..INKER
DAVE TANGUAY ....COLOURIST
DAVE TANGUAY ....LETTERER

SUPERDOG VISITS HIS FRIENDS, *THE DOG STAR PATROL!*

HAPPY FUN DAY

HAPPY

HAPPY FUN DAY

WOW! WHAT'S ALL THIS?

IT'S *FUN DAY EVE,* SILLY.

TUSKY HUSK

TAIL TERRIE

BRAINY BA

DELIVER-OUR-MAIL-CARRIER

JESSE LEON MCCANN - WRITER   **MIN S. KU** - PENCILLER
JEFF ALBRECHT - INKER   **DAVE TANGUAY** - LETTERER/COLORIST
RACHEL GLUCKSTERN - ASSOC. EDITOR   **JOAN HILTY** - EDITOR

FUN DAY?

FUN DAY IS A *GALACTIC HOLIDAY.* IT'S USHERED IN BY THE DELIVERY OF *PACKAGES* AND *CARDS* FROM ALL OVER THE GALAXY BY A JOLLY *DELIVERY MAN.*

WHO, *SANTA?*

NO, THE *INTERGALACTIC MAILMAN!*

BARK! BARK!

WOOF!

FUN DAY   HAPPY   DAY   HAPPY

YIP! YIP!

GRRR!

6

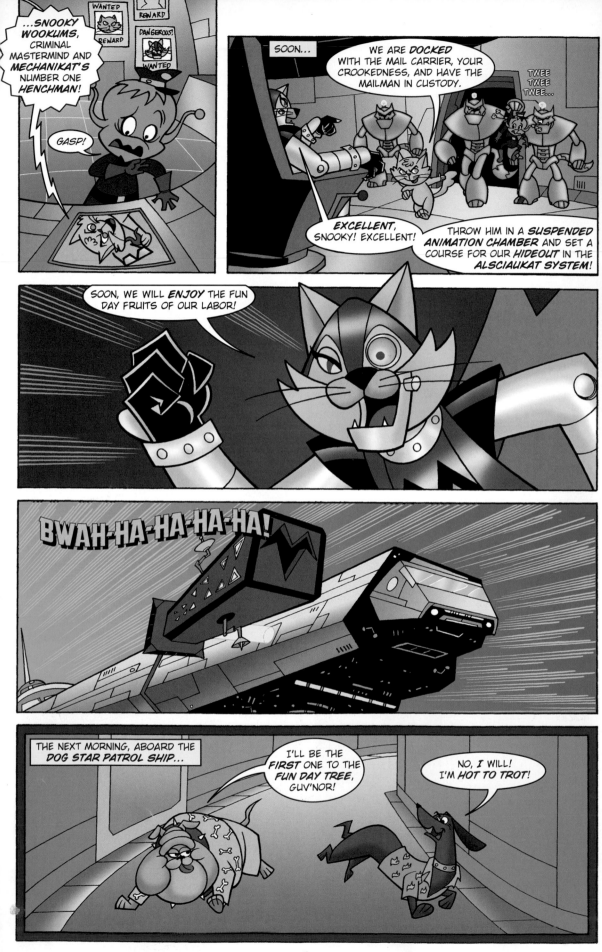

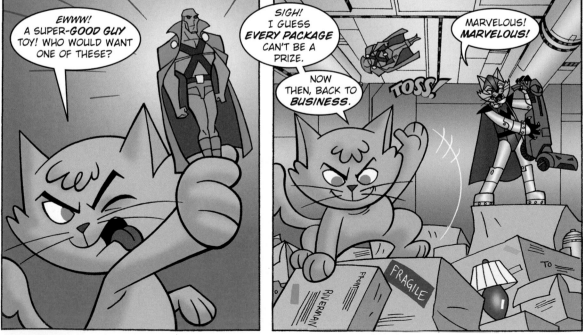

YOU BET YOUR SWEET BEPPO!

JESSE LEON McCANN — WRITER
MIN S. KU — PENCILLER
JEFF ALBRECHT — INKER
DAVE TANGUAY — LETTERER/COLORIST
RACHEL GLUCKSTERN-ASSOC. EDITOR
JOAN HILTY— EDITOR

EVERYONE KNOWS ABOUT THE FATEFUL DAY YEARS AGO ON THE DOOMED PLANET KRYPTON...

JOR-EL AND LARA SENT THEIR YOUNG SON KAL-EL TO ANOTHER WORLD TO SAVE HIM FROM KRYPTON'S DESTRUCTION...

BUT DID YOU KNOW ABOUT THIS?

A LITTLE MONKEY NAMED *BEPPO* ESCAPED KRYPTON, TOO...AS A STOWAWAY!

OOOK! JUMPSUITS! BEPPO LIKE!

WHEN THE ROCKET REACHED EARTH, BEPPO SAW HIS *NEW HOME* FOR THE FIRST TIME...

BEPPO LIKE *VERY MUCH!*

15

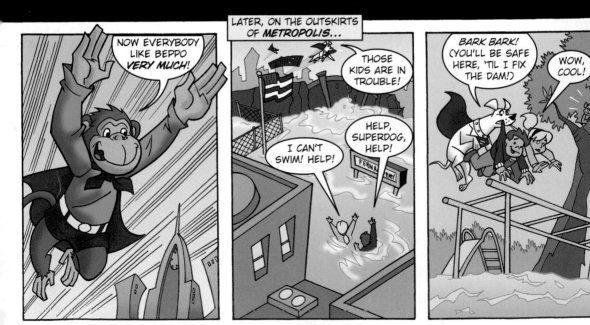

22

23

RUFF, RUFF AND AWAY!

GOODBYE!

THE END

KU ALBRECHT TANGUAY

Superdog Jokes!

WHY DOES A DOG SCRATCH ITSELF?

BECAUSE NO ONE ELSE KNOWS WHERE IT ITCHES!

WHAT DO DOGS PLAYING VIDEO GAMES SAY WHEN THEY NEED A BREAK?

PRESS PAWS!

HOW DO YOU KEEP A DOG FROM SMELLING?

HOLD ITS NOSE!

WHAT DID THE FLEA SAY TO ITS FRIEND?

SHALL WE WALK OR TAKE A DOG?

Creators

JESSE LEON MCCANN WRITER

Jesse Leon McCann is a *New York Times* Top-Ten Children's Book Writer, as well as a prolific all-ages comics writer. His credits include Pinky and the Brain, Animaniacs, and Looney Tunes for DC Comics; Scooby-Doo and Shrek 2 for Scholastic; and The Simpsons and Futurama for Bongo Comics. He lives in Los Angeles with his wife and four cats.

MIN SUNG KU PENCILLER

As a young child, Min Sung Ku dreamt of becoming a comic book illustrator. At six years old, he drew a picture of Superman standing behind the American flag. He has since achieved his childhood dream, having illustrated popular licensed comics properties like the Justice League, Batman Beyond, Spider-Man, Ben 10, Phineas & Ferb, the Replacements, the Proud Family, Krypto the Superdog, and, of course, Superman. Min lives with his lovely wife and their beautiful twin daughters, Elisia and Eliana.

DAVE TANGUAY COLOURIST/LETTERER

David Tanguay has over 20 years of experience in the comic book industry. He has worked as an editor, layout artist, colourist, and letterer. He has also done web design, and he taught computer graphics at the State University of New York.

Glossary

APPRECIATED enjoyed or valued someone or something

CONTEMPTIBLE not worthy of respect

EXPLOIT brave and daring deed

HANDIWORK works or acts done by a specific person

HENCHMAN thug or criminal subordinate

IMITATE to copy or mimic someone or something

MARVELLOUS very good or outstanding

RECOGNIZE to see someone or something and know who the person or thing is

UNINHABITED unoccupied or deserted

Visual Questions & Prompts

1. BASED ON WHAT YOU KNOW ABOUT BEPPO, WHY CAN WE SEE THROUGH THE TREES IN THIS PANEL?

WHEN THE ROCKET REACHED EARTH, BEPPO SAW HIS *NEW HOME* FOR THE FIRST TIME...

BEPPO LIKE *VERY MUCH!*

1

2. OF ALL THE SUPER-PET SUPERPOWERS THAT ARE USED IN THIS BOOK, WHICH PET'S POWER DO YOU THINK IS THE COOLEST?

FRAGILE TO:

2

3. WHY DO YOU THINK THE ARTISTS CHOSE TO ADD BRIGHT LINES BEHIND COMET IN THIS PANEL?

3

4. WHY DID BEPPO STRAND THIS BOY ON TOP OF A TELEPHONE POLE? WHAT WAS HE INTENDING TO DO, AND WHY DID HE MAKE A MISTAKE?

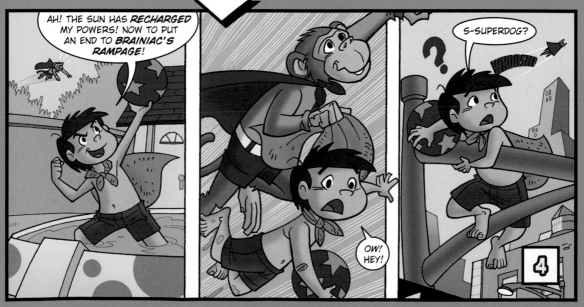

AH! THE SUN HAS *RECHARGED* MY POWERS! NOW TO PUT AN END TO *BRAINIAC'S RAMPAGE!*

OW! HEY!

S-SUPERDOG?

4